Turtles

Remember Me Series

By

Caroline Norsk

Copyright © 2014 by Caroline Norsk

All rights reserved. No part of this book may be used or reproduced in any manner whatsoever without the express written permission of the publisher except for the use of brief quotations in a book review

Image Credits: Royalty free images reproduced under license from various stock image repositories. Under a creative commons licenses.

Remember me I am a turtle.

Remember me I carry my house, which people call "carapace."

Remember me I walk very, very slow.

Remember me my babies emerge from eggs and I call my babies "sparkies."

Turtles

Remember me I go on land and in water.

Remember me I can live up to 200 years.

Remember me you can drape a scarf around my shell.

Remember me my shell is made of the same material as your fingernails.

Remember me I use only one organ to perform all my functions.

Remember me I can be your pet.

Remember me some people eat my meat in a delicious soup.

Remember me I am color blind.

Remember me I can breathe underwater.

Remember me if you find me with a duck-like feet, I live in water.

Remember me I am born near-sighted.

Remember me I can live long enough without eating.

Remember me I eat fruits and vegetables.

Remember me I sometimes eat fish, tadpoles, snails, and insects.

Remember me I am usually small but some are extraordinary, growing really large.

Remember me my shell is typically black, brown or olive green, while some are naturally colorful.

Turtles

Thank you.

Good Luck.

Made in the USA
Middletown, DE
01 May 2017